BETWEEN
A ROCK AND
A GRACE
PLACE

PARTICIPANT'S GUIDE

D0167539

CAROL KENT

Bestselling Author of *When I Lay My Isaac Down*

BETWEEN A ROCK AND A GRACE PLACE

DIVINE SURPRISES IN THE TIGHT SPOTS OF LIFE

PARTICIPANT'S GUIDE
SIX SESSIONS

ZONDERVAN.com/
AUTHORTRACKER
follow your favorite authors

ZONDERVAN

Between a Rock and a Grace Place Participant's Guide
Copyright © 2011 by Carol Kent

Requests for information should be addressed to:

Zondervan, *Grand Rapids, Michigan 49530*

ISBN 978-0-310-89033-1

Cover design: Curt Diepenhorst
Cover photography: Shutterstock® Images
Interior design: Beth Shagene

Printed in the United States of America

13 14 15 16 17 18 /DCI/ 22 21 20 19 18 17 16 15 14 13 12 11 10 9 8 7 6 5 4

CONTENTS

ABOUT THE STUDY

A WORD
FROM CAROL KENT

If you picked up this participant's guide, it no doubt means you are someone who is living in the middle of circumstances you wish were more favorable. Or, you might be gathering with a group of friends who want to encourage each other to hold on to hope and find divine surprises in the tight spots of life. Whatever your situation, I'm glad you have joined this study!

My own life was turned upside-down when my son, a graduate of the U.S. Naval Academy, was arrested for the murder of his wife's first husband. After going through two and a half years and seven postponements of his trial, he was eventually convicted of first-degree murder and sentenced to life without the possibility of parole. I know what it's like to feel "between a rock and a grace place."

One day when I was struggling with "sad mama" thoughts, my sister Jennie emailed me a verse from the Bible that captivated my heart. Even though I grew up as a preacher's kid, went to church almost every Sunday, and have read and studied the Bible throughout my life, I didn't recall hearing Romans 9:33. When Jennie shared Eugene Peterson's rendering from *The Message*, the verse came alive for me:

> Careful! I've put a huge stone on the road to Mount Zion,
>   a stone you can't get around.
> But the stone is me! If you're looking for me,
>   you'll find me on the way, not in the way.

It has now been more than a decade ago — right in the middle of my life — that I ran into a huge boulder, the likes of which I had never encountered on my lifelong walk with God. It could have been my

7

stopping place — the point at which I lost not only some of my most cherished dreams but also my faith, my joy, my purpose, and my passion to go on. Instead, I found out that the Rock in my path represented not an obstacle but an opportunity to encounter the living God in surprising, sometimes astonishing ways. As I have learned to press into the Rock in the middle of my hard places, I have discovered that I am actually in a position of safety, refuge, and grace. Year after year, God continues to transform my hard places into grace places where I discover surprising gifts of faith, mercy, contentment, praise, blessing, freedom, laughter, and adventure — tailor-made for me with his tender, loving care.

If you too feel caught in one of those tight spots that seem unusually difficult, if not unbearable, I pray that you will come to realize that the pain of being in this place need not cause you to lose hope. If you press into the Rock instead of trying to get around it, you will discover a surprise far better than a birthday or a Christmas gift. On the road that is your life right now, you can find a new way of thinking about your circumstances, as well as an astonishing experience of grace, tailor-made just for you. As you encounter God *on* the way, not *in* the way, you may come to know him as you never have before. Remember what Olympian Eric Liddell said: "Circumstances may appear to wreck our lives and God's plans, but God is not helpless among the ruins."

I'd love to stay connected to you throughout your study of *Between a Rock and a Grace Place*. You'll find regular blog updates at *www.CarolKent.org* or you can follow me at *www.twitter.com/CarolKentSpeaks*. I post encouraging quotes and updates on my speaking schedule daily. Please let me know how God is using this study in your life and how he is teaching you "to lean into the grace place."

How to Use This Guide

GROUP SIZE

Between a Rock and a Grace Place is designed to be experienced in a group setting such as a Bible study, Sunday school class, or any small group gathering. To ensure everyone has enough time to participate in discussions, it is recommended that large groups break up into smaller groups of four to six people each.

Each participant should have his or her own participant's guide, which includes notes for video segments, directions for activities and discussion questions, as well as a reading plan and optional take-home assignments to deepen learning between sessions. Although the study can be fully experienced with just the video and this participant's guide, participants are also encouraged to have a copy of the *Between a Rock and a Grace Place* book. Reading the book along with watching the video sessions provides even deeper insights that make the journey richer and more meaningful.

FORMAT OPTIONS

Between a Rock and a Grace Place can be used by groups that meet for one hour or two hours. Each group session can be completed in one hour but includes optional activities and group discussions that expand the material to accommodate groups that meet for two hours.

TIMING

The time notations — for example (20 minutes) — indicate the actual time of video segments and the suggested times for each activity or discussion. Adhering to the suggested times will enable you to complete each session in one hour. If you have additional time, you may wish to allow more time for discussion and activities.

Alternate time notations and optional activities for two-hour groups are set off with a gray background. For example:

GROUP DISCUSSION ▪ Grace in the Hardest of Places:
Surprised by Faith (5 MINUTES)

If your group meets for two hours, allow 10 MINUTES for this discussion.

In this example, one-hour groups allow 5 minutes for the discussion and two-hour groups allow 10 minutes for the discussion.

FACILITATION

Each group should appoint a facilitator who is responsible for starting the video and for keeping track of time during discussions and activities. Facilitators may also read questions aloud and monitor discussions, prompting participants to respond and assuring that everyone has the opportunity to participate.

BETWEEN-SESSIONS PERSONAL GROWTH

Maximize the impact of the course between sessions by reading the corresponding chapter in the *Between a Rock and a Grace Place* book, memorizing the suggested Scripture verse, and following through with the optional extra assignment. Setting aside just twenty to thirty minutes a day for personal study will enable you to complete the book and participant's guide by the end of the course.

SESSION 1

GRACE IN THE
HARDEST OF PLACES

SURPRISED BY FAITH

I know God will not give me anything I can't handle.
I just wish he didn't trust me so much!

Mother Teresa

WELCOME!

Welcome to session one of *Between a Rock and a Grace Place*. You
are about to begin a spiritual and personal adventure with the members of your small group. If this is your first time together as a group,
briefly introduce yourselves to each other before watching the video.
Then let's get started!

VIDEO ▪ Grace in the Hardest of Places: Surprised by Faith
(20 MINUTES)

As you watch the video, use the outline beginning on page 12 to follow along or to take notes on anything that stands out to you.

Notes

All of us long to find "the sweet spot" of God's grace when we are between a rock and a hard place.

"Careful! I've put a huge stone on the road to Mount Zion, a stone you can't get around. But the stone is me! If you're looking for me, you'll find me on the way, not in the way" (Romans 9:33).

Job's challenges: the unthinkable circumstances he encountered and how the story ended

What is faith? "Now faith is being sure of what we hope for and certain of what we do not see" (Hebrews 11:1 NIV).

A great declaration: "I keep a grip on hope. God's loyal love couldn't have run out, his merciful love couldn't have dried up. They're created new every morning. How great your faithfulness! I'm sticking with God.... He's all I've got left" (Lamentations 3:21 – 24).

When we are caught between a rock and a hard place, we are given the chance to see our human limitations and our desperate need of divine intervention.

We have a choice: Will we place ourselves in a posture of humility and complete dependence on God, or will we just "try harder" and stumble over what could be a transforming encounter with grace?

As we unwrap more of the ultimate gift of God's grace, the benefits abound:

- Eyes to see the pain of others

- A heart of compassion

- A determination to provide tangible help to others

God works best through broken people who know they do not have all the answers. He can use people who have exhausted their own resources and finally realize that negotiating the tight spots of life is not something they do by themselves.

GROUP DISCUSSION ▪ Grace in the Hardest of Places: Surprised by Faith (5 MINUTES)

If your group meets for two hours, allow 10 MINUTES for this discussion.

1. What part of the teaching impacted you most powerfully?

2. Which of the following deceptions from the enemy has been the most challenging for you and why?
   - "If you had been a better parent, this would not have happened."
   - "If you had been less busy, you could have fixed this problem before it had a negative result."
   - "If you had read your Bible more consistently and prayed more often, this would not have become a problem."

Leaning into the Grace Place

Most of us, at some point in our lives, will encounter a situation that tests our faith and makes us wonder if God is busy elsewhere and has no idea how much we are hurting. You may not have a son in prison, but your own journey has landed you between a rock and a hard place. Life is definitely different than you anticipated, and you're not sure you can cope with the obstacles you face. Answers are not forthcoming, and you may be questioning God's ways or his character.

The most important question, however, is: *How will you respond to your circumstances?* Will you withdraw from your friends and family members? Will you "ease" your way out of situations in which you hear people talk about issues of hope and faith? Or will you remain open to divine surprises in the tight spots of your life?

GROUP DISCUSSION ▪ Challenging Circumstances (5 MINUTES)

If your group meets for two hours, allow 10 MINUTES for this discussion.

1. All of us have heard people say, "I'm between a rock and a hard place." Have you been there? If so, what does that expression mean to you?

2. Looking back, when did you first encounter a life situation that stopped you in your tracks? What happened and how did it impact your faith in God?

> "The kind of faith God values seems to develop best when everything fuzzes over, when God stays silent, when the fog rolls in."
>
> Philip Yancey

GROUP DISCUSSION ▪ The Story of Job (8 MINUTES)

If your group meets for two hours, allow 15 MINUTES for this discussion.

Job had a large family — ten children! At one point he also owned seven thousand sheep, three thousand camels, one thousand cows, and five hundred donkeys. Now, that's a lot of livestock! He also had many servants to help him manage his huge estate.

Then, quite unexpectedly, everything changed. Check out his list of losses:

- His donkeys were stolen.
- Most of his faithful servants were killed.
- Lightning struck his shepherds and his sheep — and they all died.
- Marauders stole his camels.
- A fierce storm killed ALL TEN of his children.
- His health disintegrated.
- Painful, repulsive sores broke out all over his body, and he wound up sitting in a dump where he used a broken piece of pottery to scrape his oozing wounds.

Job's words reveal his plight in living color: "If my misery could be weighed, if you could pile the whole bitter load on the scales, it would be heavier than all the sand of the sea! Is it any wonder that I'm screaming like a caged cat?" (Job 6:2 – 3).

1. Job encountered unthinkable circumstances! His wife said, "Curse God and be done with it!" (Job 2:9). Have you ever experienced a time when you were furious with God? If so, did you have "a safe place" to vent your feelings?

2. Job's response is shocking in light of his trials. He said, "We take the good days from God — why not also the bad days?" (Job 2:10b). When you encounter a major crisis, is your response more like Job's or like Job's wife, or somewhere in between?

3. Read Job 42:12 – 13. Describe the latter part of Job's life.

INDIVIDUAL ACTIVITY ▪ Facing Our Fears (5 MINUTES)

Complete this activity on your own.

1. When a crisis hits, we face many fearful reactions: anxiety, stress, shock, paralysis, and sometimes anger. Carol found herself "sometimes angry, often hurt, always broken." What were some of your initial responses to your situation? Which were constructive and which were destructive?

CONSTRUCTIVE RESPONSES	DESTRUCTIVE RESPONSES

GROUP DISCUSSION ▪ Describing Faith (8 MINUTES)

If your group meets for two hours, allow 15 MINUTES for this discussion.

1. Pastor and poet Patrick Overton says, "When you have come to the edge of all light that you know and are about to drop off into the darkness of the unknown, faith is knowing one of two things will happen: There will be something solid to stand on or you will be taught to fly." Do you agree or disagree with that statement? Why?

2. What is *your* definition of faith?

3. Read Hebrews 11:1 and summarize the *biblical* definition of faith.

4. Read Lamentations 3:22 – 24. What encourages you in these verses?

5. On a scale of 1 (low) to 10 (high), how would you rate your current faith in God?

1	2	3	4	5	6	7	8	9	10

| No faith | | | | Some faith, but with uncertainty | | | | Certain that God is still in control | |

Do you think that it's okay to question your faith? Why or why not?

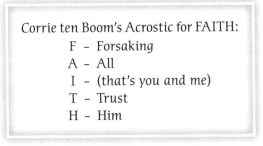

Corrie ten Boom's Acrostic for FAITH:
F - Forsaking
A - All
I - (that's you and me)
T - Trust
H - Him

GROUP DISCUSSION ▪ A Question of Attitude (5 MINUTES)

If your group meets for two hours, allow 10 MINUTES for this discussion.

Jason Kent wrote: "Mom, I hate prison. But I refuse to waste prison. I choose to believe that God still has a purpose for me in spite of what I have done and the consequences I am living with. I am committed to looking for opportunities to make a positive difference in the lives of the men around me" (*Between a Rock and a Grace Place*, p. 41).

1. Have you ever been in a difficult situation where you knew God didn't plan what took place (either due to living in a fallen world or through your own wrong choices), but you refused to waste the pain? What happened?

2. List some positive action steps we can choose for ourselves or to help others when they are between a rock and a grace place.

INDIVIDUAL ACTIVITY ▪ What I Want to Remember (2 MINUTES)

Complete this activity on your own.

1. Briefly review the outline and the notes you took while you watched this session's video.

2. In the space below, write down the most significant thing you gained in this session (from the teaching, activities, or discussions).

What I want to remember from this session ...

CLOSING PRAYER

Close your time together with prayer.

> "Faith is not simply a belief we embrace with our intellect; it is a living, breathing approach to whatever is in front of us in the here and now. Developing a faith that works in the hard places of life requires practice ... to get up every morning and put one foot in front of the other, trusting that God is still at work in our situation."
>
> Carol Kent, *Between a Rock and a Grace Place*, p. 39

EXPLORING YOUR OWN GRACE PLACE

Optional Take-Home Assignment

- You may have already read chapter 1 in the book *Between a Rock and a Grace Place.* By session two, try to read both chapters 1 and 2 in preparation for your next small group meeting.

- Memorize Hebrews 11:1 (NIV): "Now faith is being sure of what we hope for and certain of what we do not see." Write this verse on a 3 x 5 card or on a sticky note and place it where you will see it several times a day. You may discover that you will memorize the verse without even trying and it will become a permanent part of your response to God when you face difficult circumstances.

- Oswald Chambers said: "Faith is deliberate confidence in the character of God whose ways you may not understand at the time." Sometimes the best place to start rebuilding your faith is by writing out your experience of a difficult impasse that, humanly speaking, seems unfair, unreasonable, and too much to bear. Then write down where you are in your walk with God. Describe what you currently believe about his character and how that impacts your ability to hold on to your faith. If you are in too much pain to take this action step right now, that's all right. Simply acknowledging that you're in a painful place and you don't have all the answers is a good place to start, too. In fact, it can be a humble first step to being surprised by faith in the midst of an unexpected journey. A journal page — "Exploring My Grace Place" — has been provided for your personal reflections.

EXPLORING MY GRACE PLACE

ANGELS IN DISGUISE

SURPRISED BY MERCY

What did you do today that
only a Christian would have done?
Corrie ten Boom

GROUP DISCUSSION ▪ The Week in Review (5 MINUTES)

If your group meets for two hours, allow **15 MINUTES** for this discussion.

Welcome to session two of *Between a Rock and a Grace Place.* A key part of this study is sharing what you are learning with the other members of the group. Before watching this session's video teaching segment, talk about your experiences since the last meeting. For example:

- Did you meet anyone during the past week who is stuck between a rock and a hard place? If so, did you have an opportunity to share something you have already learned in this study?

- Did anyone memorize Hebrews 11:1? How has that Scripture impacted how you think about life's challenges and a biblical understanding of faith?

VIDEO ▪ Angels in Disguise: Surprised by Mercy (20 MINUTES)

As you watch the video, use the outline beginning on page 26 to follow along or to take notes on anything that stands out to you.

Notes

The kind of mercy God asks us to extend to others, particularly when they're between a rock and a hard place, sometimes requires us to dig deeply into the soil of spiritual compassion.

A religious scholar approached Jesus: "What do I need to do to get eternal life?" (Luke 10:25b)

Jesus turned the question back on the man and asked him what was written in the law. The man quoted from the Old Testament: "That you love the Lord your God with all your passion and prayer and muscle and intelligence — and that you love your neighbor as well as you do yourself" (Luke 10:27).

When scholar asked: "And just how would you define 'neighbor'?" (Luke 10:29), Jesus responded with the story of the Good Samaritan (vv. 30 – 35).

There are many definitions for mercy.

Authentic compassion and genuine mercy never say, "You poor thing! I feel sorry for you!" God's love transforms us into people who have a better way of meeting the needs of others.

Turn interruptions into divine appointments.

"If your heart is broken, you'll find God right there; if you're kicked in the gut, he'll help you catch your breath" (Psalm 34:18).

Leaning into the Grace Place

It often feels easier to *give* mercy than to receive it. But when we're in the middle of a situation we can't "fix" on our own, the tangible compassion of a fellow traveler can be a humbling and delightful surprise on our journey. Sometimes that gift of mercy comes through kind eyes instead of harsh judgment. It can come in the form of emotional or financial support, a handwritten note, or a bouquet of flowers. It can be as simple as a bag of groceries or as major as a large check. Someone sees our need, goes out of his or her way to understand our situation, and does something concrete to make sure our condition is improved. The action of a mercy-giver is often a complete surprise to the recipient. My son calls it "being like Jesus with skin on," because the result brings relief, hope, and healing. We begin to see light at the end of the tunnel, and the person who flips that switch on is our "angel in disguise."

GROUP DISCUSSION ▪ Discovering Your Comfort Zone (8 MINUTES)

If your group meets for two hours, allow 15 MINUTES for this discussion.

1. How do you define a "tight spot" in life? Have you found yourself in one that was temporarily challenging, or has it permanently altered your life?

2. When you are in a difficult situation, do you like to be left alone or do you appreciate receiving assistance from a caring person? Why?

3. Do you think it is easier to give mercy or to receive mercy? Explain.

GROUP DISCUSSION ▪ The Story of the Good Samaritan (8 MINUTES)

If your group meets for two hours, allow 15 MINUTES for this discussion.

Jesus told the story of the Good Samaritan to define "neighbor" in a whole new way. Jews and Samaritans were cultural and religious enemies during the time when Jesus taught, and the scholar testing Jesus knew this as well as anyone. Certainly, the person least likely to act mercifully toward an injured Jew would be a Samaritan. Right?

1. Describe what it would look like if you loved God with all your passion, prayer, muscle, and intelligence. What action steps would you take if you loved him that much?

2. If you were the Jewish person beaten to within an inch of your life, what would you be feeling or thinking in:
   • Verse 31

   • Verse 32

   • Verses 33 – 35

> "A friend hears the song in my heart and sings it to me when memory fails."
>
> Anonymous

3. Why do you think Jesus used this story to convey the importance of loving one's neighbor?

4. In the story of the Good Samaritan, the man who received help from an unlikely source was "surprised by mercy." He was in great need, and he received extraordinary care. Have you ever received mercy from an unexpected source or from an unlikely person? What happened and how did it impact your life?

INDIVIDUAL ACTIVITY ▪ A Personal Evaluation (5 MINUTES)

Complete this activity on your own.

1. Write a brief paragraph about a time when you were able "to be Jesus with skin on" to another person.

2. On a scale of 1 (low) to 10 (high), how would you rate your response to the needs of others?

1	2	3	4	5	6	7	8	9	10

Fine letting others step in		Some mercy, but guarded		Quick to meet the needs of others

Why would you say you typically behave this way?

GROUP DISCUSSION ▪ Defining Mercy (8 MINUTES)

If your group meets for two hours, allow 15 MINUTES for this discussion.

1. Mercy has many definitions:

   a. to ease distress or pain

   b. to show compassion to another

   c. to forgive a wrong

   d. to receive a kindness from someone who has more power or resources than you do

   Which of these descriptions means the most to you? Describe a time in your life when you experienced one of these forms of mercy.

2. Sometimes we feel more comfortable showing mercy to people who are financially challenged or to those who are facing health problems or whose difficulties are due to circumstances entirely beyond their control. But when someone is struggling with an addiction or has committed a crime, or when their situation is in some other way "socially unacceptable," we often don't know how to respond. Share some practical ways the body of Christ can reach out to people who may feel unworthy of receiving help.

3. If you had time to read chapter 2 of the *Between a Rock and a Grace Place* book, what did you learn from Gail and Brian Knarr's story? What aspect of the way people demonstrated mercy to them impacted you the most? What can our churches learn from the Knarrs' difficult experience?

> "Never worry about numbers. Help one person at a time, and always start with the person nearest you."
> Mother Teresa

GROUP DISCUSSION ▪ What's the Difference? (5 MINUTES)

If your group meets for two hours, allow 10 MINUTES for this discussion.

1. Describe the difference between pity and mercy.

2. Carol Kent was surprised by the mercy of Nurse Betty toward her son. What did you learn from this story?

INDIVIDUAL ACTIVITY ▪ What I Want to Remember (2 MINUTES)

Complete this activity on your own.

1. Briefly review the outline and the notes you took while you watched this session's video.

2. In the space provided on page 34, write down the most significant thing you gained in this session (from the teaching, activities, or discussions).

What I want to remember from this session ...

CLOSING PRAYER

Close your time together with prayer.

> "I've discovered that one of the most important ways God is 'right there' in times of need is through the kindness and mercy of other people.... And he tells us to do the same for the hurting people we find on the roads we travel."
>
> Carol Kent, *Between a Rock and a Grace Place*, p. 61

EXPLORING YOUR OWN GRACE PLACE

Optional Take-Home Assignment

- Read chapter 3 in the *Between a Rock and a Grace Place* book in preparation for your next small group meeting.

- Memorize Psalm 34:18 (NIV): "The LORD is close to the broken-hearted and saves those who are crushed in spirit." Write this verse on a 3 x 5 card or on a sticky note and place it where you will see it several times a day. Speak the verse out loud when you are at home or in the car alone. Meditate on the meaning. Write a response to this question: *How has God used brokenness in the past to draw me closer to him?*

- This session began with a quote from Corrie ten Boom: "What did you do today that only a Christian would have done?" Jesus himself said, "I was hungry and you fed me, I was thirsty and you gave me a drink, I was homeless and you gave me a room, I was shivering and you gave me clothes, I was sick and you stopped to visit, I was in prison and you came to me" (Matthew 25:35 – 36). List the people within your sphere of influence who are having a difficult time right now. Next to each name write down one thing you could do to show mercy to that individual or family. Remember, mercy doesn't need to cost a lot. Mercy sees a need, evaluates the resources available, and chooses to get involved in a personal, tangible way. How can you be "Jesus with skin on" to someone in your path this week?

The Needs of My Family/Friends	How Can I Show Mercy?

- Use the page 36 journal space to record what God is teaching you.

EXPLORING MY GRACE PLACE

_____

_____

_____

_____

_____

_____

_____

_____

_____

_____

_____

_____

_____

_____

_____

_____

_____

_____

_____

_____

Longing
for a Better Life

SURPRISED BY CONTENTMENT

> The happiness which brings enduring worth to life is not
> the superficial happiness that is dependent on circumstances.
> It is the happiness and contentment that fills the soul even
> in the midst of the most distressing circumstances and the most
> bitter environment. It is the kind of happiness that grins
> when things go wrong and smiles through the tears.
>
> **Dr. Billy Graham**

GROUP DISCUSSION ▪ The Week in Review (5 MINUTES)

If your group meets for two hours, allow 15 MINUTES for this discussion.

Welcome to session three of *Between a Rock and a Grace Place*. A key part of your personal and spiritual growth in this study is sharing your journey with each other. Before watching this session's video teaching segment, talk about your experiences since the last meeting. Conversation starters:

- We ended last session with a challenge from Corrie ten Boom: "What did you do today that only a Christian would have done?" Divide into groups of two or three and share one thing you did in the past week to show mercy to someone else. What was the result? (If your group is less than six people, stay together for the sharing.)

- Your memory verse was Psalm 34:18 (NIV): "The LORD is close to the brokenhearted and saves those who are crushed in spirit." Did you have a chance to share that verse with someone in your life this past week, or did you experience God's comfort to your own heart during a difficult time?

VIDEO ▪ Longing for a Better Life: Surprised by Contentment
(20 MINUTES)

As you watch the video, use the outline that begins below to follow along or to take notes on anything that stands out to you.

Notes

When you are living between a rock and a grace place, it's easy to look around and see people with better circumstances — and suddenly you realize you feel very discontent with your own life situation.

God loves to interject divine surprises into our lives!

Definition of contentment: a feeling of satisfaction with our own possessions, status, or situation in life

Paul's words of wisdom in 2 Corinthians 12:7 – 10; he was given "the gift of a handicap."

Three things steal our contentment:
- Jealousy
- Stress
- Comparison

Paul's bold statement in Philippians 4:11 – 13

God's promise: Hebrews 13:4

Philippians 4:6 – 7

"Give your entire attention to what God is doing right now, and don't get worked up about what may or may not happen tomorrow. God will help you deal with whatever hard things come up when the time comes" (Matthew 6:34).

Ask God to guard your heart and mind as you intentionally practice this discipline. Contentment is not just a feeling, and it need not be dependent upon personal circumstances.

Leaning into the Grace Place

Sometimes it's easiest to understand what contentment is when we're not thinking about it. When "all is well" in our little world, we generally feel calm and can go with the flow. However, when we get the unexpected, middle-of-the-night phone call telling us to come to the hospital immediately, or we discover a spouse has been unfaithful, or our child has been arrested, or we miscarry the baby we longed for, or we have a life-altering accident, or we are diagnosed with cancer, our easy peace dissolves into internal chaos. If our equilibrium isn't restored fairly quickly, we can become riddled with discontent.

Sometimes we wonder: *Does God even care about what has happened? Why does he allow bad things to happen to people who are trying to live the way he wants them to?* Rationally we understand that we live in a fallen world where there's plenty of injustice, sickness, and sorrow. But sometimes we get stuck in the quagmire of self-pity, and that's when it's easy to compare our reality to the more "perfect" reality of someone else. Then we're filled with the poison of envy and resentment on top of having to deal with our difficult situation. What a mess!

GROUP DISCUSSION ▪ Longing for a Better Life: Surprised by Contentment (5 MINUTES)

If your group meets for two hours, allow 15 MINUTES for this discussion.

1. How do you define the word "contentment"?

2. On a daily basis, how do these factors impact your contentment?
   - Relationships with your friends, spouse, or children
   - Finances
   - Job situation
   - Spiritual relationship

3. On a scale of 1 (low) to 10 (high), how do you rate your sense of contentment right now?

1	2	3	4	5	6	7	8	9	10
Dissatisfied				Okay, but striving for more peace					Totally content

4. When you are discontent, how do you process your emotions? Do you keep your feelings bottled up inside, or do the people around you know you are struggling?

> "Experiencing contentment in my current circumstances is a daily choice, and some days are much harder than others. But I find that my times of pain lead me to my most intimate times of prayer and communion with God."
>
> Jason Kent, quoted in *Between a Rock and a Grace Place*, p. 78

GROUP DISCUSSION ▪ Divine Surprises (5 MINUTES)

If your group meets for two hours, allow 10 MINUTES for this discussion.

1. Carol shared the story of finding the unexpected Christmas gift on her porch at a time when she needed encouragement. Think about a time in your life when God surprised you in a significant way. What was the surprise? How did it impact your faith? How did it encourage you?

2. Have you ever had an opportunity to surprise someone who needed to be reminded of God's care and provision? What was the result?

GROUP DISCUSSION ▪ The Apostle Paul: His Challenge (5 MINUTES)

If your group meets for two hours, allow 10 MINUTES for this discussion.

Read 2 Corinthians 12:7 – 10 aloud.

1. What do you think Paul's "thorn in the flesh" was?

2. What benefits did Paul receive from this challenging issue?

3. When Paul begged God to remove this handicap, what answer did he receive?

4. Describe a time in your life when God did not answer your prayer for relief from a problem or a challenge. Was your response like Paul's when he said, "That is why, for Christ's sake, I delight in weaknesses, in insults, in hardships, in persecutions, in difficulties. For when I am weak, then I am strong" (2 Corinthians 12:10 NIV)? If not, how *did* you respond?

INDIVIDUAL ACTIVITY ▪ Contentment Stealers (5 MINUTES)

Complete this activity on your own.

1. Write a sentence or two about how your contentment has been stolen in the past by any of the following feelings:

   • Jealousy

   • Stress

   • Comparison

GROUP DISCUSSION ▪ Discontent (8 MINUTES)

If your group meets for two hours, allow 15 MINUTES for this discussion.

1. Gene shared his feelings about being jealous when he observed the grown son of his best friend having a "normal" life. He was happy for his friend but sad for himself. Do you ever struggle with envy and, if so, how does it impact your sense of contentment? What action steps could you take to get back on track personally and spiritually?

2. How does mounting stress impact your sense of contentment? Has there been a time when, in the middle of an outburst, you realized "the real issue" was far different from "the single incident" that put you over the edge emotionally? What happened?

3. What techniques do you use for avoiding the pitfalls of comparison?

INDIVIDUAL ACTIVITY ▪ Cultivating Inner Peace (5 MINUTES)

Complete this activity on your own.

1. Read the following Scripture verses and summarize the main points:

- Philippians 3:11 – 13

- Hebrews 13:14

- 1 Timothy 6:6 – 7

> "Worry is a cycle of inefficient thoughts whirling around a center of fear. Worry doesn't empty tomorrow of its sorrow. It empties today of its strength."
>
> Corrie ten Boom

GROUP DISCUSSION ▪ Developing an Eternal Perspective

(5 MINUTES)

If your group meets for two hours, allow 10 MINUTES for this discussion.

1. The much-loved author C. S. Lewis once said: "If I find in myself a desire which no experience in this world can satisfy, the most probable explanation is that I was made for another world." What does this statement mean to you?

2. As you consider Jason Kent's prison experiences and the story you read in the book about Cathy Gallagher's quest for a fulfilling job, what do you think the two of them are learning about true contentment?

INDIVIDUAL ACTIVITY ▪ What I Want to Remember (2 MINUTES)

Complete this activity on your own.

1. Briefly review the outline and the notes you took while you watched this session's video.

2. In the space below, write down the most significant thing you gained in this session (from the teaching, activities, or discussions).

What I want to remember from this session ...

CLOSING PRAYER

Close your time together with prayer.

EXPLORING YOUR OWN GRACE PLACE

Optional Take-Home Assignment

- Read chapters 4 and 5 of the book *Between a Rock and a Grace Place* in preparation for your next small group meeting.

- Memorize Matthew 6:34 (NIV): "Therefore do not worry about tomorrow, for tomorrow will worry about itself. Each day has enough trouble of its own." Write this verse on a 3 x 5 card or on a sticky note and place it where you will see it several times a day. Speak the verse out loud several times a day. Meditate on the meaning. Write a response to this question: *How will it benefit me and the people around me if I stop worrying about what might happen in the future?*

- *The Message* version of Matthew 6:34 says: "Give your entire attention to what God is doing right now, and don't get worked up about what may or may not happen tomorrow. God will help you deal with whatever hard things come up when the time comes." Write out a prayer to God listing your worries and your needs. Ask him for wisdom and peace, and invite him to guard your heart and mind this week as you intentionally practice contentment.

- Use this session's journal page to record your response, prayer, or anything else God is teaching you.

EXPLORING MY GRACE PLACE

THE SECRET POWER
OF GRATITUDE

SURPRISED BY THANKSGIVING

Thanksgiving puts power into living,
because it opens the generators
of the heart to respond gratefully,
to receive joyfully, and to react creatively.

C. Neil Strait

GROUP DISCUSSION ▪ The Week in Review (5 MINUTES)

If your group meets for two hours, allow 15 MINUTES for this discussion.

Welcome to session four of *Between a Rock and a Grace Place.* A key part of personal and spiritual growth is sharing your journey with each other. Before watching this session's video teaching segment, let's talk about what we are learning.

- What insights did you get out of last session's study on contentment?

- Did you recognize any of the stealers of contentment (jealousy, stress, or comparison) rising up in a personal situation since the last time we met? If so, how did you respond?

- Was there a victory you experienced in applying what you learned in the last session?

- How did the memory verse impact your thinking?

VIDEO ▪ The Secret Power of Gratitude: Surprised by Thanksgiving (20 MINUTES)

As you watch the video, use the outline that begins below to follow along or to take notes on anything that stands out to you.

Notes

A "perfect" Thanksgiving reunion, followed by a crisis that turned life upside down

The story of King Jehoshaphat's unusual battle (2 Chronicles 20:4 – 33)

- Three allied enemies declare war on the king and his people.

- The king asks God for guidance and instructs the people to fast and pray.

- Taking courage in the priest's assurance of victory, the king appoints a choir to march ahead of the troops and to sing: "Give thanks to the LORD; his love endures forever" (v. 21 NIV).

- When they arrive at the Valley of Berakah they discover the soldiers of the opposing armies had already killed each other.

- Jehoshaphat lived a life characteristic of his father Asa, pleasing to God — no detours, no dead-ends. However, he failed to remove all the pagan shrines and the people never fully committed themselves to God.

Carol's mother instructed her to memorize 1 Thessalonians 5:16 – 23, reminding her to choose a heart of thanksgiving in the hard places of life.

There's a surprising treasure when we verbalize praise to God based on his character, not on our negative circumstances.

Jason's lessons on giving thanks and on recognizing grace places in his current circumstances

Carol's answered prayers for her son

Leaning into the Grace Place

In our growing up years we were taught to be courteous and polite. It was natural to say "thank you" when someone extended a kindness, spoke up on our behalf, or gave us a gift. However, all of us have discovered it's much more challenging to have a grateful heart when the threads of suffering weave unexpected crises into our carefully made designs for life. I know God is honored when we quit complaining and start thanking him in the middle of our struggles, but when faced with ongoing disappointment and loss upon loss, it's hard to remember to maintain a spirit of gratitude. I'm grateful to have a wise and godly mother, who reminds me that voicing thanks to God leads to feeling grateful — and it's hard to be in a bad mood when I have a grateful heart.

GROUP DISCUSSION ▪ The Secret Power of Gratitude: Surprised by Thanksgiving (8 MINUTES)

If your group meets for two hours, allow 15 MINUTES for this discussion.

1. Most of us grew up in a home where either our parents gave praise and gratitude often or were quick with negative comments and criticism. On a scale of 1 (low) to 10 (high), how often did you hear praise or thanks from either or both of your parents?

1	2	3	4	5	6	7	8	9	10

I only heard negative responses.	They occasionally voiced praise.	They expressed praise often.

2. How did your parents' verbal responses affect you in your growing-up years? How has it influenced your current relationships?

3. What are you particularly grateful for today?

4. When you experience deep disappointment or get devastating news, which of the following reactions are you most likely to have: fear, anger, or denial? Why do you think you tend to respond in this way?

> "The best technique I have for fighting depression is making myself think of all the things I am thankful for. If I think and write about my blessings, I realize there's always something to be thankful for."
>
> Jason Kent, quoted in *Between a Rock and a Grace Place*, p. 100

GROUP DISCUSSION ▪ The Story of King Jehoshaphat's Unusual Approach to Battle (5 MINUTES)

If your group meets for two hours, allow 10 MINUTES for this discussion.

Think back to the story of King Jehoshaphat from the video segment or, time permitting, read it in 2 Chronicles 20:1 – 35.

1. What challenge did the king face?

2. What was his first response?

3. Describe the prophetic words of the priest Jahaziel when he was moved by God's Spirit to speak.

4. How did King Jehoshaphat respond to the words of Jahaziel?

5. What were the king's instructions the following morning? What benefits did he and his troops experience when their first response to a negative situation was giving thanks to God?

6. What did the king, choir, and army find in the Valley of Berakah? How were all the people of Judah surprised and rewarded when their leaders started a "battle" in such an unconventional way?

"The supreme challenge to anyone facing catastrophic loss involves facing the darkness of the loss on the one hand, and learning to live with renewed vitality and gratitude on the other.... Loss can diminish us, but it can also expand us.... Loss can function as a catalyst to transform us."

Jerry Sittser, *A Grace Disguised*

INDIVIDUAL ACTIVITY ▪ An Honest Evaluation (5 MINUTES)

Read 2 Chronicles 20:32 – 33 and answer the following questions on your own.

1. Describe in a sentence or two what you learned from the example of King Jehoshaphat in these two verses?

2. On a scale of 1 (low) to 10 (high), how often do you respond to bad news with thanksgiving to God?

1	2	3	4	5	6	7	8	9	10
Never				Not right away, but eventually					I give thanks in everything.

3. There are many kinds of battles in our lives — fortunately, most are not in a war zone or behind prison bars. Think of a situation in which someone else's discipline of offering thanksgiving and praise not only broke their own chains of negativity but also liberated others in some way.

GROUP DISCUSSION ▪ True Gratitude (5 MINUTES)

If your group meets for two hours, allow 10 MINUTES for this discussion.

1. True gratitude consists of two elements: first, showing appreciation for the benefits that are received, and second, bringing joy to others by supplying comfort to them during their time of

need. Which of the two elements of this definition are you best at expressing and why?

2. Is the element of gratitude you didn't select hard for you to convey in a tangible way? If it is, why do you think that is so?

"The blessing of gratitude is like a boomerang. When it flies out of a truly grateful heart, it hovers momentarily above the receiver, blessing its recipient, and then makes a 180-degree turn back into the life of the one who offered thanks."

Rebecca Barlow Jordan, *40 Days in God's Blessing*

GROUP PROJECT ▪ The Essence of Thanksgiving (8 MINUTES)

If your group meets for two hours, allow 15 MINUTES for this discussion.

1. Take turns reading each of the following Scriptures. After each passage is read, jot down its core message:

   • Psalm 118:28

• Colossians 3:15 – 16

• 1 Corinthians 15:57

• Philippians 4:6 – 7

• 1 Thessalonians 5:16 – 18

2. Chapter 4 of *Between a Rock and a Grace Place* recounts the story of twin girls, Sarah and Kendall — one with autism and the other without. There are times in our lives when Scripture's command "In everything give thanks" (1 Thessalonians 5:18 NASB) appears to be not only challenging, but impossible. What did you learn from mother Jill's story that will help you benefit from her example?

INDIVIDUAL ACTIVITY ▪ What I Want to Remember (2 MINUTES)

Complete this activity on your own.

1. Briefly review the outline and the notes you took while you watched this session's video.

2. In the space below, write down the most significant thing you gained in this session (from the teaching, activities, or discussions).

What I want to remember from this session ...

CLOSING PRAYER

Close your time together with prayer.

> "When I have a thankful heart, I find joy welling up that splashes into the lives of others. I'm learning the secret power of giving thanks — even when I don't feel like it!"
>
> Carol Kent

EXPLORING YOUR OWN GRACE PLACE

Optional Take-Home Assignment

- Read chapter 6 of the book *Between a Rock and a Grace Place* in preparation for your next small group meeting.

- Memorize 1 Thessalonians 5:16 – 18 (NIV): "Be joyful always; pray continually; give thanks in all circumstances, for this is God's will for you in Christ Jesus." Write this passage on a 3 x 5 card or on a sticky note and place it where you will see it several times a day. Speak the passage aloud as you read it. Meditate on the meaning. Write a response to this question: *How would the people around me benefit if I put these verses into practice?*

- This study is about leaning into "the grace place" and finding faith, safety, comfort, contentment, joy, and blessing — even when life doesn't turn out as expected. Irish bishop and historian Richard P. C. Hanson writes, "Grace means the free, unmerited, unexpected love of God, and all the benefits, delights, and comforts which flow from it." On your journal page, list five things you have to be thankful for in the middle of an unexpected or unwanted change in your life. Pray through your list every day this week, verbalizing your thanks to God for any benefit, however small, of your unforeseen circumstances.

EXPLORING MY GRACE PLACE

WHY DO YOU WEEP?

SURPRISED BY JOY

I've survived because I've discovered a new
and different kind of joy that I never knew existed—
a joy that can coexist with uncertainty
and doubt, pain, confusion, and ambiguity.

Tim Hansel, *You Gotta Keep Dancin'*

GROUP DISCUSSION ▪ The Week in Review (5 MINUTES)

If your group meets for two hours, allow 15 MINUTES for this discussion.

Welcome to session five of *Between a Rock and a Grace Place*. A key part of personal and spiritual growth is sharing your journey with each other. Before watching this session's video teaching segment, talk about your experiences since the last meeting.

- How does a thankful attitude impact your thinking, your behavior, and your relationship with God?
- What is the main thing you learned from the example of King Jehoshaphat in the last session?
- What challenges did you experience as you worked on applying the truths from last session?

VIDEO ▪ Why Do You Weep? Surprised by Joy (20 MINUTES)

As you watch the video, use the outline beginning on page 66 to follow along or to take notes on anything that stands out to you.

Notes

Let's get real

- Have you ever put on a plastic smile when your heart is breaking?
- Have you gone to a meeting or to church and acted like everything is "fine"?
- Are you so vulnerable that you never cover up your sadness?

Carol intentionally surrounds herself with joy-givers and tries to connect with people who bring humor into her life.

One of the things that rob us of joy is the memory of what we perceive to be "better days."

Mary Magdalene knew much about sorrow, but because of Jesus, she also learned much about joy.

- He freed her from seven demons.

- She had the joy of being part of the team of people who served Jesus during his public ministry.

- She experienced the heartache of witnessing the crucifixion of a close friend.

- She was the first to see the risen Lord at a time in history when women weren't even considered legitimate witnesses.

Mary's two powerful experiences: an empty tomb moment and an empty tomb reality

Jason's definition of joy: celebrating God's powerful hand at work even when we don't understand why he allows certain things to happen

Surprised by joy: the story of Tammy Wilson and Matt Rodriguez

> "We could never learn to be brave and patient if there were only joy in the world."
>
> Helen Keller

Leaning into the Grace Place

Most of us experience joy when we observe people we love celebrating good news or special occasions. It's easy to feel joyful when a baby is born, or when people gather to honor someone at a birthday, graduation, or anniversary party. It's also natural to feel a relaxed, "all-is-right-with-the-world" kind of happiness when we find a quiet place at a beach or in the mountains where we can breathe deeply and take in the splendor of God's creation. Sometimes we find joy in a special chair in our home where we curl up with a good book and relish the pleasure of some quiet time to ourselves. But we might not be as quick to recognize or appreciate the other "flavors" of joy — those that are harder won and sometimes enjoyed only after we've stood bereft at what appears to be an empty "tomb" in our life.

GROUP DISCUSSION ▪ Surprised by Joy (5 MINUTES)

If your group meets for two hours, allow 10 MINUTES for this discussion.

1. What part of the video teaching had the greatest impact on you?

2. When you are going through difficult experiences, how important is it to intentionally keep humor as part of your life? Do you have one specific person who is your "off-the-wall" funny friend, or do you have several people in your life who provide much-needed laughter?

INDIVIDUAL ACTIVITY ▪ Evaluating Your Response to Life (5 MINUTES)

Complete this activity on your own.

1. How often do you experience joy?

1	2	3	4	5	6	7	8	9	10
Never			Seldom		Occasionally		Often		Several times a day

2. In general, has your joy in past years come during specific times of celebration *or* as an "abiding" type of joy no matter what circumstances you are in?

3. Finish this sentence: *Joy, for me, is* _____

_____

_____.

GROUP DISCUSSION ▪ Investigating Joy (5 MINUTES)

If your group meets for two hours, allow 15 MINUTES for this discussion.

1. How do you define "joy"? (Feel free to refer to the notes you wrote during the individual activity.)

2. What brings you happiness?

3. Are joy and happiness the same thing for you? If there's a difference, what sets joy apart from happiness?

4. Is there a special place, person, or occasion that always brings joy to your heart and refreshment to your soul? Explain.

GROUP DISCUSSION ▪ What the Bible Says about Joy (5 MINUTES)

If your group meets for two hours, allow 15 MINUTES for this discussion.

1. Take turns reading each of the following Scriptures aloud and write a take-home truth based on each:

   • Psalm 4:7

   • Psalm 126:5

   • James 1:2

   • Romans 15:13

   • Psalm 30:11

2. Which of these verses describes what you have personally experienced about true joy? Or are you still trying to find your joy? That's okay. Being honest with God about your journey is the first step in making progress toward a level of intimacy with him that leads to joy.

> "Life need not be easy to be joyful; joy is not the absence of trouble but the presence of Christ."
>
> William Vander Hoven

INDIVIDUAL ACTIVITY ▪ The Story of Mary Magdalene (5 MINUTES)

Complete this activity on your own.

1. Once Mary Magdalene met Jesus, she was never the same. Which of her experiences do you identify with most? Write a sentence or two about each aspect of her life that parallels your own growing journey with Christ.

   • Jesus set her free from a past filled with anguish.

- She was part of Jesus' inner circle in which friends bonded and got to know the Master intimately.

- She had an "empty tomb moment" when it appeared that he was gone.

- She experienced the "empty tomb reality" when she discovered that Jesus was alive and powerfully at work in her life.

GROUP DISCUSSION ▪ Responding to Mary Magdalene's Encounter with Jesus (5 MINUTES)

If your group meets for two hours, allow 10 MINUTES for this discussion.

1. Describe how Mary Magdalene must have felt after being freed from seven demons.

2. Mary was part of the "road team" of people who traveled with Jesus. Have you ever taken a road trip with close friends? What kinds of bonding experiences take place when you travel with friends and how do you think these travels impacted Mary's friendship with Jesus?

3. After the crucifixion, Mary saw where Jesus was laid in a tomb. Two mornings later he was gone. Have you ever had an "empty tomb moment" in your life when it felt like God had no interest in your pain and no longer appeared present in your circumstances? What happened?

4. When Jesus spoke Mary's name, she recognized his voice and experienced "the empty tomb reality." He was there all the time, but she had not recognized him for who he was. What is your most recent experience of discovering the presence of God in your circumstances at an urgent time of need?

GROUP DISCUSSION ▪ Choosing Joy (5 MINUTES)

If your group meets for two hours, allow 10 MINUTES for this discussion.

1. Both Diana Pintar and Jason Kent have experienced situations that could have permanently stolen their joy, but they discovered great delight in unexpected places. What did you learn from their stories about cultivating joy?

2. On a scale of 1 (low) to 10 (high), how do you rate your sense of joy during this time in your life? Why?

1	2	3	4	5	6	7	8	9	10

I've lost my joy.   My joy comes and goes, but I'm okay.   I am delighting in life!

> "Joy, for me, is knowing as concretely as I know my name and my birthday that God is real and that he loves me personally, and that I'm never alone and he can be trusted with my heart."
>
> Jason Kent, quoted in *Between a Rock and a Grace Place*, p. 142

INDIVIDUAL ACTIVITY ▪ What I Want to Remember (2 MINUTES)

Complete this activity on your own.

1. Briefly review the outline and the notes you took while you watched this session's video.

2. In the space below, write down the most significant thing you gained in this session (from the teaching, activities, or discussions).

What I want to remember from this session ...

CLOSING PRAYER

Close your time together with prayer.

> "Our shattered dreams are never random. They are always a piece in a larger puzzle, a chapter in a larger story. Pain is a tragedy. But it's never only a tragedy.... The journey to joy takes us through shattered dreams."
>
> Dr. Larry Crabb, *Shattered Dreams*

EXPLORING YOUR OWN GRACE PLACE

Optional Take-Home Assignment

- Read chapters 7 and 8 of the book *Between a Rock and a Grace Place* in preparation for the final small group session.

- Memorize Psalm 30:5b (NKJV): "Weeping may endure for a night, but joy comes in the morning." Write this verse on a 3 x 5 card or on a sticky note and place it where you will see it several times a day. Speak the verse aloud as you read it. Meditate on its meaning.

- In the journal space on page 78, write responses to these questions: *How does Psalm 30:5 give you hope? In what specific situations will you choose joy this week?*

EXPLORING MY GRACE PLACE

LIBERTY
OF THE HEART

SURPRISED BY FREEDOM

Freedom is an inside job.

Sam Keen

GROUP DISCUSSION ▪ The Week in Review (5 MINUTES)

If your group meets for two hours, allow **15 MINUTES** for this discussion.

Welcome to our final session of the *Between a Rock and a Grace Place* study. A key part of personal and spiritual growth is sharing your journey with each other. Before watching this session's video teaching segment, talk about your experiences since the last meeting.

- What insights did you discover from the life of Mary Magdalene in session five?

- What challenges or victories did you experience in applying what you learned last time?

- What questions do you have for other members of the group?

VIDEO ▪ Liberty of the Heart: Surprised by Freedom (20 MINUTES)

As you watch the video, use the outline beginning on page 80 to follow along or to take notes on anything that stands out to you.

Notes

All of us have longings for (1) significance, (2) security, (3) intimacy, (4) success, and (5) spirituality.

Disappointment comes and we wish for the happier or more peaceful life we once enjoyed.

No matter their source, disappointments keep us in a prison of our own making.

Carol and Gene's disappointment: the exhaustion of all appeals at both the state and federal levels in their son's case, followed by a denial of the necessary waiver for a clemency hearing

The secret to "liberty of the heart": purpose and meaning in the place I'm in right now!

"The Master, GOD, has given me a well-taught tongue, so I know how to encourage tired people. He wakes me up in the morning, wakes me up, opens my ears to listen as one ready to take orders" (Isaiah 50:4).

It's His-story and he allows us to play starring roles in his spectacular drama. The best part of the story unfolds in the next scene (the one we haven't lived yet).

"I run in the path of your commands, for you have set my heart free" (Psalm 119:32 NIV).

Peter's story of being set free (Acts 12:5 – 9) reveals:

- He had personal failures he never dreamed would be part of his biography.
- He discovered his human limitations in following and honoring Jesus in no way limited Jesus' grace toward him.
- We can experience freedom on the inside, even when we blow it in our walk with God. Jesus extended grace to Peter and he went forward to become a "fisher of men" and a "rock" in the foundation of the church.

A glorious surprise: Jesus understood the depth of Peter's love for him. He not only forgave Peter, but he also entrusted him with the monumental job of establishing the Christian church on earth.

For those who love Christ, personal sin and failure need not spell the end of our story.

Leaning into the Grace Place

Freedom is something most of us take for granted. We make decisions about what our daily activities will be, and we move around at will. Freedom on the inside involves the ability to be at peace in the middle of circumstances that, humanly speaking, have the potential to make us feel confined or without a sense of control over the outcome of our lives. That kind of freedom can be hard won, but along the way to attaining it we are often given opportunities to experience divine surprises and unexpected benefits.

GROUP DISCUSSION ▪ Inner Freedom (5 MINUTES)

If your group meets for two hours, allow 15 MINUTES for this discussion.

1. What does the title of this chapter — "Liberty of the Heart" — mean to you?

2. In 2 Corinthians 3:17 (NASB), Paul writes: "Now the Lord is the Spirit, and where the Spirit of the Lord is, there is liberty." How is it possible to live in the middle of unresolved issues and tight spots and still experience inner freedom?

3. In what ways have you experienced this kind of freedom in your own life?

> "The only way to live in this adventure — with all its danger and unpredictability and immensely high stakes — is in an ongoing, intimate relationship with God."
>
> John Eldredge, *Wild at Heart*

INDIVIDUAL ACTIVITY ▪ Facing Personal Challenges (5 MINUTES)

Complete this activity on your own.

1. Which of the following longings have you struggled with most? Write a sentence of explanation for the two that give you the most intense challenge.

   • Significance

   • Security

   • Intimacy

- Success

- Spirituality

2. How do you usually deal with your disappointments and unful-filled expectations?

GROUP DISCUSSION ▪ Dealing with Emotions (5 MINUTES)

If your group meets for two hours, allow 10 MINUTES for this discussion.

1. From the following list, describe your typical response when you have been wronged by someone:
   - I am a "hot reactor." I get my emotions out on the table and no one has to guess what I'm feeling.
   - I am a "slow boiler." I hide my feelings inside and say, "No problem," pretending everything is okay. But there's a bubbling cauldron of emotion welling up, and it eventually explodes.
   - I stuff and deny my emotions, not wanting anyone to guess I'm upset or feel angry and resentful. I rarely let anyone see my feelings.

2. How do you move in the direction of inner freedom when you want to lean into "the grace place" and make a biblical decision?

GROUP DISCUSSION ▪ Peter's Story (5 MINUTES)

If your group meets for two hours, allow 10 MINUTES for this discussion.

1. Peter is an intriguing New Testament Bible character. Which of the following details from his life do you most identify with? Why?

   • He was energetic and spontaneous — sometimes speaking or acting impulsively, without thinking about the consequences.

   • He said he loved Jesus enough to die for him, yet he denied Jesus three times — treating one of his best friends without loyalty or respect. When his faith was put to the test, he failed miserably.

   • Jesus understood how much Peter loved him, and in spite of the disciple's failures, Jesus extended extravagant forgiveness. Peter was also given the opportunity to do great ministry (which, in his case, was to establish the Christian church).

> "To live by grace means to acknowledge my whole life story, the light side and the dark. In admitting my shadow side I learn who I am and what God's grace means."
>
> Brennan Manning

GROUP DISCUSSION ▪ Surprised by Freedom (5 MINUTES)

If your group meets for two hours, allow 15 MINUTES for this discussion.

1. This session began with a quotation by Sam Keen: "Freedom is an inside job." Do you agree or disagree with this statement? If you agree, share a time in your life when you experienced the reality of freedom on the inside.

2. Jason Kent writes about having freedom on the inside despite living in a maximum-security prison. How might you apply the lessons he's learned so that you may experience the same kind of inner peace, even in the face of deep disappointments or having no tangible reason to hope for positive change?

3. Psalm 119:32 (NIV) says: "I run in the path of your commands, for you have set my heart free." If you feel comfortable doing so, tell about a time in your life when you experienced the truth of this verse.

4. In session five Carol shared the story of Tammy Wilson and Matthew Ben Rodriguez and the miracle of forgiveness that set them both free. (You've also read their letters in chapters 7 and 8 in preparation for this session.) Tammy endured an experience most of us will never face — the violent loss of her mother that forever changed her life. What have you learned from Tammy's story, and how can you apply it in your life?

"When suffering shatters the carefully kept vase that is our lives, God stoops to pick up the pieces. But he doesn't put them back together as a restoration project patterned after our former selves. Instead, he sifts through the rubble and selects some of the shards as raw material for another project — a mosaic that tells the story of redemption."

Ken Gire, *The North Face of God*

INDIVIDUAL ACTIVITY ▪ Choosing Forgiveness (5 MINUTES)

Complete this activity on your own.

1. Write out your own definition of "forgiveness."

2. Then fill in these blanks and turn your words into a prayer: Lord Jesus, I really need to forgive _____. My emotions of [name them here] _____ _____ have kept me in a prison of my own making. I confess all wrongdoing and wrong thinking on my part to you, and I ask for your wisdom about what steps to take next that will move me in the direction of restoration, redemption, and true liberty of the heart. Amen.

GROUP DISCUSSION ▪ The Wrap-Up (5 MINUTES)

If your group meets for two hours, allow 15 MINUTES for this discussion.

1. Which of the six sessions of this study has been the most helpful to you?

   • Grace in the Hardest of Places: Surprised by Faith
   • Angels in Disguise: Surprised by Mercy
   • Longing for a Better Life: Surprised by Contentment
   • The Secret Power of Gratitude: Surprised by Thanksgiving
   • Why Do You Weep? Surprised by Joy
   • Liberty of the Heart: Surprised by Freedom

2. What was the most important thing you learned from Jason Kent's letters?

3. What is the action step God wants you to take as a result of participating in this study?

CLOSING PRAYER

Close your time together with prayer.

"Jesus nailed it when he said, 'I came so they can have real and eternal life, more and better life than they ever dreamed of' (John 10:10). Life instead of death. Hope instead of despair. A new kind of living — harder, but better than before. Richer because of the pain. Maddening because we hate the process. Inner change instead of outward pretending. Life. Pure and simple. It's a choice. It's a new kind of normal."

Carol Kent, *A New Kind of Normal*

EXPLORING YOUR OWN GRACE PLACE
Optional Take-Home Assignment

- Memorize Psalm 119:32 (NIV): "I run in the path of your commands, for you have set my heart free." Write this verse on a 3 x 5 card or on a sticky note and place it where you will see it several times a day. Speak the verse aloud as you read it. Meditate on its meaning.

- Write a letter to God on the journal page, telling him where you are in your journey toward embracing his grace. List the divine surprises you have encountered along the way — ones that may have seemed like roadblocks at the time. What unexpected treasures have you discovered, and how have you experienced God's mercy as you have said yes to him?

- What shape does the challenge to "Seize the day!" take in your life right now? Read the following Scriptures and summarize them in a way that helps you articulate the adventure God is calling you to live out, perhaps in very surprising ways!

Jeremiah 29:11

Psalm 32:8

Joshua 1:9

Proverbs 2:1 – 5

EXPLORING MY GRACE PLACE

To schedule Carol Kent to speak at your event,

go to www.CarolKent.org.

For information on the nonprofit organization Carol and her husband, Gene, have founded to help inmates and their families, go to www.SpeakUpforHope.org.

Between a Rock and a Grace Place

Divine Surprises in the Tight Spots of Life

Carol Kent, Bestselling Author of When I Lay My Isaac Down

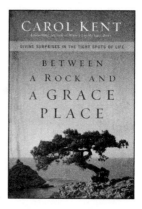

Carol Kent and her husband, Gene, are now living what some would call a heartbreaking life — their son, Jason, a young man who initially had so much promise, is now living out a life sentence for murder in a maximum security prison. All their appeals have been exhausted at both the state and federal levels — humanly speaking, they have run out of options.

But despite their hopeless situation, Carol and her husband live a life full of grace. Kent reveals how life's problems become fruitful affliction where we discover the very best divine surprises, including peace, compassion, freedom, and adventure. Through the Kents' remarkable ongoing journey, Jason's riveting letters from behind bars, and true "grace place" stories from the lives of others, *Between a Rock and a Grace Place* reveals that when seemingly insurmountable challenges crash into our lives, we can be transformed as we discover God at work in ways we never imagined.

With vulnerable openness, irrepressible hope, restored joy, and a sense of humor, Carol Kent helps readers to find God's "grace places" in the middle of their worst moments.

Available in stores and online!

Share Your Thoughts

With the Author: Your comments will be forwarded to
the author when you send them to *zauthor@zondervan.com*.

With Zondervan: Submit your review of this book
by writing to *zreview@zondervan.com*.

Free Online Resources at
www.zondervan.com

Zondervan AuthorTracker: Be notified whenever your favorite
authors publish new books, go on tour, or post an update
about what's happening in their lives at www.zondervan.com/
authortracker.

Daily Bible Verses and Devotions: Enrich your life with daily
Bible verses or devotions that help you start every morning
focused on God. Visit www.zondervan.com/newsletters.

Free Email Publications: Sign up for newsletters on Christian
living, academic resources, church ministry, fiction, children's
resources, and more. Visit www.zondervan.com/newsletters.

Zondervan Bible Search: Find and compare Bible passages in
a variety of translations at www.zondervanbiblesearch.com.

Other Benefits: Register to receive online benefits like
coupons and special offers, or to participate in research.

ZZONDERVAN®

ZONDERVAN.com/
AUTHORTRACKER
follow your favorite authors